Wallets Demystified

T.S. AVINI

Wallets Demystified

Store and Secure Your Crypto Like a Pro

by T.S. AVINI

Table of Contents

Chapter 1: Introduction to Cryptocurrency Wallets

In the rapidly evolving financial landscape of the 21st century, understanding cryptocurrency wallets is an essential skill for anyone looking to engage with digital assets effectively and securely.

At the heart of this revolution sits the cryptocurrency wallet—a multifaceted tool that not only serves as a gateway to accessing and managing digital currency but also as a custodian of personal financial empowerment. This chapter aims to demystify the enigmatic world of cryptocurrency wallets, setting the stage for deeper exploration throughout this book.

Cryptocurrency, in its essence, represents a new paradigm for currency, diverging significantly from traditional fiat systems. Unlike conventional money, which is tangible and stored in physical wallets or within the secure confines of bank accounts, cryptocurrencies are entirely digital.

They rely on decentralized ledger technology known as blockchain, which ensures transparency and security through a system that validates and records transactions across a network of computers worldwide. Within this digital ecosystem, cryptocurrency wallets emerge not as physical entities but as software or hardware solutions designed to store and manage cryptographic keys vital for transactions in digital currencies.

What is a Cryptocurrency Wallet?

A cryptocurrency wallet is not akin to a physical wallet but is better compared to a keyring—a tool that manages access to your digital wealth.

At its core, a wallet is a program or device that generates, stores, and manages a pair of cryptographic keys crucial for transacting cryptocurrencies: the public key and the private key.

The **public key** acts like an account number or an address on the blockchain. It's something you can share openly with others to receive funds. Think of it as a PO box number—it's how others send you mail, or in this case, cryptocurrency.

The **private key**, however, is akin to a signature. It is the secret string of data that allows you to access and spend your cryptocurrencies. It must remain confidential and secure; anyone with access to your private key has the ability to control your digital funds.

In real life, It is fundamental to understand that cryptocurrencies are not stored in the wallet itself—hence the term can be somewhat misleading. Instead, the wallet maintains the keys needed to interact with blockchain transactions.

The cryptocurrency itself remains on the blockchain, a distributed ledger continuously updated with new transactions across a chain of blocks. Your wallet effectively provides the means to view the balance, make transactions, and connect with the blockchain network.

Types of Cryptocurrency Wallets

Navigating the landscape of cryptocurrency wallets necessitates understanding the different wallet types available, each catering to distinct preferences and security needs.

Broadly, wallets can be categorized as hot wallets and cold wallets.

Interestingly enough, **Hot Wallets**: These are wallets connected to the internet and offer ease of use through their accessibility and user-friendly interfaces.

They are conducive to regular trading and transactions but at the expense of heightened vulnerability to cyber threats. Hot wallets manifest as:.

- **Web Wallets**: Accessible via browsers, these wallets are convenient for quick transactions.

Major exchanges offer them, but their vulnerability to phishing and hacking requires careful vigilance.

- **Mobile Wallets**: Designed for smartphones, these apps provide a balance between convenience and security, enabling users to manage their cryptocurrencies on the go.

- **Desktop Wallets**: Installed on personal computers, they offer enhanced security over web wallets, particularly if the computer is well-protected against malware and intrusions.

Cold Wallets: These are offline wallets, regarded for their security. By minimizing internet connectivity, they significantly reduce the risk of online threats.

- **Hardware Wallets**: Physical devices resembling USB drives, hardware wallets securely store private keys offline.

They require physical possession and action, making them a preferred choice for long-term investors keen on security.

At first glance, - **Paper Wallets**: These are printouts of your public and private keys.

Being entirely offline, they offer ideal security but demand meticulous safeguarding from physical damage and loss.

Each wallet type has its trade-offs.

Individuals engaged in frequent, small-scale transactions might prefer hot wallet solutions, whereas those holding substantial currency amounts for extended periods might opt for the security of cold storage solutions.

Security Considerations

It's worth noting that Security in the realm of cryptocurrency is paramount. The decentralized nature of cryptocurrencies demands personal responsibility in securing one's digital assets.

A myriad of threats, from hacking and phishing attacks to hardware malfunctions, can endanger your cryptocurrency holdings. Some fundamental practices to bolster security include:.

- **Safeguarding Private Keys**: Never share your private key with anyone. Treat it with utmost confidentiality.

- **Using Strong Passwords**: Ensure that any access points, whether wallet apps or exchange accounts, are fortified with complex, unique passwords.

- **Enabling Two-Factor Authentication (2FA)**: This additional security layer adds resilience against unauthorized access.

- **Regular Backups**: Periodically backing up wallet data can recovery in the event of device failure.

- **Staying Vigilant Against Phishing Scams**: Always verify the authenticity of websites before inputting any credentials, and remain cautious of any unsolicited communications requesting your wallet details.

Conclusion

Cryptocurrency wallets are indispensable instruments for navigating the expanses of digital currencies. Each decision regarding the type of wallet and security measures aligns with personal preferences and financial goals.

Understanding the intricacies of these wallets enables users to not only manage their assets efficiently but also safeguard them effectively against potential threats. As you delve deeper into the subsequent chapters of this book, you will acquire a comprehensive understanding of how to maximize the utility of cryptocurrency wallets, ensuring that you keep your digital assets not only accessible but secure, always adhering to best practices in a constantly evolving digital landscape. In this financial revolution, your wallet is not just a tool—it is your fortress.

Chapter 2: The Evolution of Digital Storage: From Hard Drives to Blockchain

In our pursuit of storing information securely and efficiently, humanity has traversed a fascinating journey, one that has seen the transformation of storage media from the clunky and tangible to the ethereal and digital.

This evolution is not only a testament to technological innovation but also a reflection of our growing demand for convenience, capacity, and, more notably in recent times, security. As we delve into the history and development of digital storage, we shall better understand the genesis of current blockchain technology and its implications for crypto wallets.

The saga begins with magnetic storage technologies, which marked the initial leap from paper records to digital ones. The first commercially viable digital storage device was the hard drive, introduced by IBM in 1956.

These devices were initially cumbersome, with a single drive occupying space equivalent to that of two large refrigerators and boasting a paltry five megabytes of storage capacity. Over the decades, however, advancements in miniaturization and materials science dramatically reduced their size while exponentially increasing their capacity, eventually culminating in hard disks with terabytes of storage, small enough to fit in the palm of one's hand.

At first glance, The next breakthrough came with the development of solid-state drives (SSDs). Unlike hard drives, SSDs have no moving parts, relying instead on flash memory to store data.

Introduced in the late 1980s, SSDs offered significantly faster read and write speeds, greater reliability, and reduced energy consumption. As SSD technology advanced, it rapidly overtook traditional hard drives in performance, rendering them obsolete in many high-performance settings. The progress from magnetic to solid-state storage marked a maturation in our approach to data storage — one that emphasized speed, efficiency, and reliability.

However, even as physical storage media evolved, the need for storing, sharing, and transferring vast quantities of data spurred the development of cloud storage solutions. Pioneers like Amazon Web Services and Dropbox ushered in an era where data could be seamlessly accessed from anywhere in the world.

Cloud storage offered the unprecedented advantage of scalability and redundancy, ensuring data protection against hardware failures. This shift from local to cloud storage illustrated a key evolution in perception: that data could transcend physical constraints, existing wherever and whenever needed.

While these innovations redefined data accessibility and reliability, they did little to address privacy and security. Incremental improvements in encryption and data protection measures were launched in tandem, but a considerable gap persisted—a gap that would become alarmingly evident with increasing incidents of data breaches and cyber attacks.

The cloud's centralized nature, while beneficial in many aspects, also posed a significant vulnerability. There was an ever-growing demand for a paradigm-shifting approach to data security, one that could offer ownership and control back to the individual user. Enter blockchain technology.

Blockchain emerged from the computational and cryptographic brilliance encapsulated in Satoshi Nakamoto's 2008 whitepaper, culminating in the birth of Bitcoin, the first decentralized cryptocurrency.

At its heart, blockchain provided a novel approach to digital storage and transactions, solving the double-spending problem without the need for a trusted third party. It was this decentralized, immutable ledger technology that laid the foundation for an entirely new philosophy in data storage and security.

Unlike previous storage solutions, blockchain operates on a decentralized framework wherein data is encrypted and distributed across an extensive network of nodes.

Each node holds a copy of the entire blockchain, enabling transparency and restorability in the event of data corruption at any single point. This architecture ensures that no single entity can exercise control over the data, significantly enhancing security against traditional forms of tampering and failure.

Further augmenting blockchain's appeal is its immutability.

Once data is recorded in a blockchain, altering it is nearly impossible without consensus across the network, providing long-desired protection against unauthorized manipulation. This immutability position blockchain as a reliable method for recording transactions, agreements, and credentials, which traditional methods could not guarantee.

As blockchain technology matured, its application transcended beyond cryptocurrencies and morphed into various domains, with smart contracts and decentralized applications (dApps) gaining prominence.

Ethereum played a pivotal role in this diversification, introducing a programmable blockchain that facilitated automated transactions upon meeting predefined conditions. Coupled with cryptographic wallets, blockchain applications began revolutionizing a plethora of fields, including finance, supply chain, healthcare, and more.

In the realm of cryptocurrency storage, blockchain technology offers unparalleled security through crypto wallets, which can be categorized into software-based hot wallets and hardware-based cold wallets.

Hot wallets, connected to the internet, provide convenience for transactions, while cold wallets, stored offline, ensure heightened protection. Each employs a cryptographic key mechanism, where public keys serve as the address for transactions, while private keys act as the safeguard, much like the combination to a safe.

The evolution of digital storage, from tangible hard drives to the abstract blockchain, underscores a shift in priorities.

The necessity for increased security, enhanced privacy, and improved control over personal data has driven the quest for innovation, giving rise to blockchain—a technology that epitomizes these values.

Let's not forget, As we navigate this ongoing evolution, it is crucial to understand the historical context out of which blockchain emerged.

It provides valuable insights into the strengths and constraints of contemporary digital storage solutions and highlights why blockchain stands as a pivotal development. In comprehending this transformation, we equip ourselves to better utilize and adapt to these technologies, ensuring that we store and secure our digital assets with the highest efficacy.

In this chapter, we have explored how blockchain, as a revolutionary storage technology, satisfies the modern demands of security, certitude, and decentralization. Together, these attributes empower individuals to hold authority over their digital presence like never before, setting a precedent for the future.

The days of relegating our most precious data to the mercy of intermediaries are fading. With blockchain, we enter an era empowered by self-sovereignty and unparalleled security—an era where your crypto wallet is not just a tool, but a testament to a revolutionary leap in digital autonomy.

Chapter 3: Understanding the Basics: What is a Crypto Wallet?

As we venture further into the cryptoverse, one of the most essential tools you will encounter is the crypto wallet. Yet, the term "wallet" can be misleading for those new to cryptocurrency, as it conjures images of a leather pouch used to carry cash and cards.

In the realm of digital currencies, however, a wallet operates on quite a different premise. It is prudent to understand that a crypto wallet is not a vessel for actual coins or tokens, but rather a sophisticated tool for managing cryptographic keys.

The Nature of Crypto Wallets

I've seen this happen before: At its core, a crypto wallet is a software application or a physical device that allows users to interact with blockchain networks.

It enables the storage, sending, and receiving of cryptocurrencies. But contrary to the notion of literal storage, cryptocurrencies never actually leave the blockchain.

Cryptocurrencies exist on a blockchain—a publicly-accessible, decentralized ledger system.

A crypto wallet manages a user's private and public keys, which are the key elements that facilitate the relationship with the blockchain. Essentially, your wallet helps prove ownership and authorize transactions on the network.

Public and Private Keys: The Heart of the Matter

In real life, To understand crypto wallets, one must first grasp the concept of public and private keys.

These are not physical keys but are instead complex alphanumeric codes that serve distinct purposes.

The **public key** is analogous to an email address.

It can be shared openly and used by others to send you cryptocurrencies. However, while anyone can send crypto to a public key, they cannot access the fund it represents without the corresponding private key.

The **private key** is the cryptographic secret known only to you.

Think of it as your password or PIN number, but with one crucial distinction—the loss of your private key usually results in the permanent loss of access to your funds. It serves as the exclusive means of signing transactions and proving ownership of the assets associated with your public key on the blockchain.

Types of Crypto Wallets

Understanding the variety of crypto wallets available is critical for choosing the right one for your needs.

Broadly, wallets can be categorized into two major types: custodial and non-custodial, each with distinctive subcategories.

1. **Custodial Wallets**

Custodial wallets are managed by third-party services, typically cryptocurrency exchanges like Coinbase or Binance. In this scenario, the institution holds your private keys, and therefore the control of your crypto assets.

This is akin to storing your money in a bank. Custodial wallets are user-friendly and require less technical knowledge, making them popular among beginners.

However, they come with a trade-off: you're entrusting another party with the security of your assets.

This can be risky, as exchanges are prime targets for hacks. Therefore, while convenient, custodial wallets may not offer the highest level of security for those seeking full control over their cryptocurrencies.

2. **Non-Custodial Wallets**

Believe it or not, Non-custodial wallets, on the other hand, give you full control over your private keys.

These wallets are often used by those who prioritize security and autonomy. Here are some popular forms of non-custodial wallets:.

- **Software Wallets**: These are applications that can be installed on your computer or smartphone. They are accessible and user-friendly, allowing easy access to your crypto from anywhere.

Examples include Exodus and Electrum. However, they are connected to the internet, making them potentially vulnerable to online threats.

- **Hardware Wallets**: Physical devices specifically built for securing cryptocurrencies. These wallets store your private keys offline, or "cold," making them highly resistant to hacking attempts.

Prominent examples are Ledger and Trezor. Due to their security features, they are recommended for storing larger amounts of cryptocurrency.

- **Paper Wallets**: An old-school method of writing down your keys or printing them out on a piece of paper.

While offline and immune to digital attacks, they are vulnerable to physical damage or loss.

- **Web Wallets**: These are browser-based wallets that can be accessed from any internet-connected device.

While convenient, they carry the risk of phishing attacks and malware.

Security Implications

As strange as it sounds, The choice of a crypto wallet has significant implications for the safety of your digital assets.

For custodial solutions, the onus is on the provider to offer robust security measures. Still, it's critical to research an exchange's track record on security breaches, regulatory compliance, and user feedback.

For non-custodial wallets, the responsibility lies with you. Protecting your private key is paramount.

This involves not only keeping it secret but also creating backups to safeguard against loss. Many people opt for hardware wallets as they provide the highest level of security combined with ease-of-use for signing transactions.

Conclusion

Interestingly enough, A crypto wallet is more than just a storage solution; it acts as your gateway to the blockchain, empowering you to engage with the digital economy.

By grasping the significance of safeguarding your private keys and understanding the various types of wallets available, you are equipped to make educated decisions on how to store and manage your cryptocurrency assets effectively.

Whether you opt for the convenience of a custodial wallet or the independence of a non-custodial one, remember that the cornerstone of cryptocurrency lies in personal sovereignty and security.

Choose wisely, and your crypto endeavors will be both insightful and secure.

Chapter 4: Different Types of Crypto Wallets: Hot vs. Cold

In the dynamic world of cryptocurrencies, safeguarding your assets is paramount. A critical aspect of this security involves understanding the different types of crypto wallets available and their unique characteristics.

At the heart of cryptocurrency storage lies a fundamental dichotomy: hot wallets versus cold wallets. Each serves distinct purposes with unique advantages and pitfalls. This chapter delves deeply into these two categories, providing an authoritative analysis to empower you in making informed decisions about where and how to store your crypto assets.

Understanding the Basics

I've seen this happen before: Before we dive into the details, let's establish what a crypto wallet is.

At its core, a cryptocurrency wallet is a device, software, or service that stores the public and/or private keys for cryptocurrency transactions. Beyond the mere act of storing, these wallets facilitate the sending and receiving of cryptocurrencies through blockchain networks while managing public addresses.

Definition and Dynamics of Hot Wallets

Hot wallets are digital currency storage solutions that maintain a connection to the internet. They are known for their convenience and accessibility.

This connectivity makes them ideal for users who frequently trade cryptocurrencies or make regular transactions. Examples of hot wallets include mobile wallets, desktop wallets, and web-based wallets. Popular hot wallets often come as mobile apps or browser plugins, such as MyEtherWallet, MetaMask, and the mobile app Bread.

Advantages of Hot Wallets

1.

Ease of Use: Hot wallets are user-friendly, usually designed with intuitive interfaces that make them accessible even to cryptocurrency novices. Their existence in the digital realm allows for instantaneous transactions without the need to transfer assets from a physical device.

2.

Convenience: The most significant advantage of hot wallets is their convenience. With internet access, users can manage and transact cryptocurrencies readily from anywhere in the world, enabling them to react quickly to market fluctuations.

In real life, 3.

Integration with Exchanges and Services: Many exchanges and crypto services have integrated wallets, allowing for seamless transfers between trading accounts and wallets, thereby facilitating quick buying, selling, or staking of cryptocurrencies.

Drawbacks of Hot Wallets

1. **Security Risks**: The primary downside of hot wallets is their vulnerability to cyber attacks.

Being connected to the internet exposes them to potential hacks, phishing attacks, and malware. If an adversary gains access to your hot wallet, they can siphon off your funds with little to no recourse for recovery.

I've seen this happen before: 2.

Reliance on Third-party Services: Many hot wallets are provided by third-party services, which pose risks in terms of reliability and security. For instance, if a company suffers a server breach or goes out of business, wallet users might find their assets compromised or inaccessible.

Nature and Nuance of Cold Wallets

Cold wallets, contrastingly, are offline storage solutions. These wallets are not connected to the internet, making them significantly more secure against online threats.

Cold wallets are ideal for the long-term storage of cryptocurrencies that are not meant for daily transactions. Examples include hardware wallets like Ledger and Trezor, as well as paper wallets and even physical coins embedded with crypto keys.

Advantages of Cold Wallets

1. **Superior Security**: The foremost benefit of cold wallets is security.

By being offline, cold wallets are immune to typical online threats such as malware, phishing, and hacking attempts. This makes them ideal for storing large amounts of cryptocurrency or assets that you don't intend to move frequently.

2.

Control over Private Keys: Cold wallets often provide complete control over private keys, without relying on third-party services. This autonomy increases security as the keys are stored completely offline and in some cases, only accessible to the user physically holding the device or printed document.

3.

Resilience to External Failures: Unlike hot wallets, cold wallets are not reliant on servers or internet services that may fail. As such, they are often seen as a more reliable method for long-term cryptocurrency storage.

Drawbacks of Cold Wallets

1.

Lack of Convenience: Cold wallets can be cumbersome for traders who need frequent access to their assets, since they often necessitate additional steps to bring a wallet online for transactions. This can include physically connecting a hardware wallet to a computer or manually inputting information from a paper wallet.

2.

Physical Risks: While cold wallets protect against digital theft, they can be susceptible to physical risks such as loss, theft, or damage. For example, a hardware wallet can be misplaced, and a paper wallet can be destroyed in a fire or flood.

3. **Expense**: Some cold wallet solutions, particularly hardware wallets, come with upfront costs, which can be a barrier for casual or small-scale investors.

Hybrid Solutions and Best Practices

To be honest, Given the pros and cons of each wallet type, many cryptocurrency investors opt for a hybrid approach, utilizing both hot and cold wallets to balance security with accessibility.

For instance, an investor might use a hot wallet for day-to-day transactions and a cold wallet for storing the bulk of their portfolio.

Best practices include keeping a minimal amount of cryptocurrency in hot wallets to limit potential exposure to security breaches, while using cold storage for reserve funds.

It's also wise to regularly update wallet software, use strong and unique passwords, and enable two-factor authentication where possible.

Conclusion

In conclusion, the decision between using a hot or cold wallet ultimately hinges on your unique needs as a cryptocurrency user. An astute understanding of the strengths and vulnerabilities of each will guide you in securing your digital assets effectively.

By incorporating a considered combination of both wallet types, and adhering to best practices, you can enhance both the security and efficiency of your crypto management strategy. As you embark on your crypto journey, remember that a well-informed approach to wallet choice is foundational to storing and securing your assets like a seasoned professional.

Chapter 5: An In-Depth Look at Software Wallets

In the vast ecosystem of cryptocurrency, understanding the various tools at your disposal is paramount to navigating securely and efficiently. Software wallets, also known as digital wallets, are among the critical tools that offer a blend of convenience and security to cryptocurrency aficionados.

In this chapter, we will dissect the complexities of software wallets, exploring their types, functionality, advantages, and potential pitfalls. Our goal is to equip you with the knowledge needed to utilize these wallets like a seasoned professional.

What Are Software Wallets?

In real life, Software wallets are applications or programs that enable users to store and manage their cryptocurrency assets digitally.

Unlike hardware wallets, which are physical devices, software wallets exist in a digital format and can be installed on your computer, mobile device, or used via web browsers. They serve as the interface to interact with the blockchain network, allowing you to perform transactions, monitor balances, and manage your private keys.

Fundamentally, software wallets store your private and public keys, offering you a means to interact with blockchain networks.

The private key is what allows you to authenticate and authorize transactions, while the public key is akin to an address that people can use to send you cryptocurrency.

Types of Software Wallets

There are three primary types of software wallets: desktop wallets, mobile wallets, and web wallets.

Each comes with its own set of features, conveniences, and security considerations.

Desktop Wallets

Desktop wallets are software programs downloaded and installed on a personal computer or laptop. They offer a high degree of control and security since you have direct access to your keys on your device.

Examples of popular desktop wallets include Electrum, Exodus, and Atomic Wallet. These wallets often come equipped with robust features like multi-signature support, encryption, and backup options.

The primary advantage of desktop wallets is that they are less susceptible to cyber threats compared to web wallets, as long as the computer itself is secure.

However, the downside is the risk of losing your funds if viruses or malware compromise your system. It is vital to keep your operating system updated and protect it with antivirus software to mitigate these risks.

Mobile Wallets

Mobile wallets are applications installed on smartphones or tablets.

They are designed for users who need access to their cryptocurrency on the go. Mobile wallets like Trust Wallet, Mycelium, and BRD offer user-friendly interfaces tailored to smaller screens and allow for quick transactions.

One of the major benefits of mobile wallets is the convenience they offer, allowing you to pay with cryptocurrency at merchants or conduct peer-to-peer transactions directly from your device.

However, this convenience comes at a potential cost to security, as mobile devices are more prone to loss, theft, or being hacked. It is essential to protect your mobile wallet with strong passwords, biometric authentication, and regular device updates.

Web Wallets

Web wallets, or online wallets, are hosted on the cloud and are accessible through web browsers.

Platforms such as Coinbase Wallet and Binance Trust Wallet operate as web-based services. These wallets are convenient because they allow access from any device with an internet connection.

Let's not forget, While web wallets provide easy accessibility, they are also at increased risk of cyber attacks like phishing and hacking.

Using reputable platforms with strong security features, including two-factor authentication (2FA), can mitigate some of these risks. However, you must remain vigilant against scams and unauthorized access by ensuring you access these services through secure, official websites.

Advantages of Software Wallets

1.

Convenience and Accessibility: Software wallets allow for seamless access to your cryptocurrencies from multiple devices. Whether you are at home or on the move, you can perform transactions with relative ease.

I've seen this happen before: 2.

User-Friendly Interfaces: Many software wallets come with straightforward, intuitive interfaces, making them suitable for beginners and experienced crypto users alike. Features such as transaction history, real-time coin value tracking, and integrated exchange services enhance the user experience.

3.

Feature-Rich: Advanced functionalities like coin exchange, portfolio management, and staking (earning interest on held cryptocurrencies) are often integrated into software wallets, providing a comprehensive solution to managing digital assets.

4.

Frequent Updates and Community Support: Software wallets benefit from regular updates, ensuring they are equipped to handle the latest security threats. Additionally, a robust community often provides support, tutorials, and forums to enhance user knowledge and security practices.

Security Considerations

While software wallets offer numerous benefits, their security largely hinges on user practices and the device's security. Here are crucial considerations to keep in mind:

- **Backups:** Regularly back up your wallet's private keys and recovery phrases.

Store these backups in secure, offline locations to prevent loss due to device failure or theft.

To be honest, - **Strong Authentication:** Use strong, unique passwords for your wallets, and enable two-factor authentication where possible.

This adds an additional layer of security by requiring an extra step of identification beyond just a password.

- **Secure Devices:** Ensure your devices have updated antivirus software, firewalls, and system updates to protect against malicious threats.

- **Caution Against Phishing Scams:** Be wary of phishing scams that aim to steal your credentials. Always double-check URLs and avoid clicking on suspicious links.

- **Use Reputable Software:** Only download wallets from reputable sources and ensure that software integrity is maintained.

Research the wallet's reputation and security history before installation.

Conclusion

Software wallets are an indispensable component in the realm of cryptocurrency management, striking a balance between accessibility and security. Understanding the different types—desktop, mobile, and web—enables users to select the best option according to their needs and circumstances.

By adopting robust security practices, users can protect their digital assets while benefiting from the convenience and advanced features that software wallets offer. As with any tool in the crypto world, vigilance and continuous learning are key to turning challenges into opportunities and ensuring safe navigation through the complex landscape of digital currencies.

Chapter 6: Navigating Hardware Wallets: A Physical Approach

In the rapidly evolving world of cryptocurrencies, safeguarding your digital assets is paramount. As hackers and cybercriminals have become more sophisticated, the need for robust security measures has intensified.

Enter hardware wallets—a tangible solution to the intangible world of digital finance. This chapter will guide you through the nuts and bolts of hardware wallets, explaining their nature, benefits, and practical use in securing your crypto assets like a pro.

Understanding Hardware Wallets

Interestingly enough, Hardware wallets are physical devices designed to keep your cryptocurrency private keys offline, safeguarding them from the prying eyes of the internet.

Unlike software wallets, which operate on devices connected to networks and are potentially vulnerable to hacks, hardware wallets provide an extra layer of security by storing your keys in a secure, offline environment. Think of a hardware wallet as a fortified vault for your digital wealth.

A typical hardware wallet contains a microcontroller, which allows it to securely generate and store private keys.

It also features a small screen to review and verify transactions, and connects to your computer or smartphone via USB or Bluetooth. This combination of hardware-based security and limited connectivity significantly reduces the risk of unauthorized access.

The Benefits of Using Hardware Wallets

Many people don't realize this, but 1. **Enhanced Security**: The primary advantage of a hardware wallet is its unparalleled security.

Since your private keys never leave the device, they are isolated from your internet-connected computer or smartphone. This air-gap approach greatly minimizes the risk of cyber attacks, phishing attempts, and malware infections.

2. **User-Friendly Interface**: Despite their sophisticated technology, most hardware wallets are designed with user-friendliness in mind.

Even those who aren't technically inclined can navigate through the setup and transaction verification processes with ease. The intuitive interface on devices' screens allows users to see and approve every transaction manually.

3.

Compatibility and Adaptability: Hardware wallets support a wide range of cryptocurrencies, from Bitcoin and Ethereum to lesser-known altcoins. Many wallets also integrate seamlessly with popular software wallets and third-party applications, offering you flexibility and convenience in managing your assets.

Let's not forget, 4. **Backup and Recovery Options**: A critical aspect of hardware wallets is their reliable backup feature.

During initial setup, users are prompted to write down a recovery seed—a series of 12 to 24 randomly generated words. This seed acts as a failsafe, enabling you to recover your funds should your wallet be lost, damaged, or stolen.

Choosing the Right Hardware Wallet

The market offers a variety of hardware wallets, each with unique features tailored to different user needs.

Some of the most reputable brands include Ledger, Trezor, and KeepKey. When selecting a wallet, consider the following factors:.

To be honest, - **Security Features**: Look for wallets that offer advanced security mechanisms, such as secure element chips, PIN protection, and passphrase support.

These features add layers of security, ensuring your funds remain inaccessible to unauthorized users.

- **Supported Currencies**: Ensure that the wallet supports the cryptocurrencies that you own or plan to purchase.

Wallets differ in their compatibility, and using one that supports a broad range of assets helps streamline your cryptocurrency management.

- **User Experience**: A good user interface is crucial.

The device should be easy to set up and use, even for those without technical expertise. Consider wallets with touchscreen interfaces, as they often enhance user experience.

To be honest, - **Company Reputation and Community Support**: Opt for wallets manufactured by reputable companies with a track record of reliability and strong customer support.

Engaging with active user communities can also provide valuable insights and troubleshooting tips.

Setting Up Your Hardware Wallet

Setting up a hardware wallet typically involves a few key steps. Here's a general guide to help you get started:

Believe it or not, 1.

Purchase from a Reputable Source: Always buy your hardware wallet from an official website or authorized reseller to ensure authenticity and avoid counterfeit devices.

2.

Unbox and Verify: Upon receiving your wallet, carefully unbox it and check for any signs of tampering. Most manufacturers have tamper-evident seals which provide an additional layer of assurance.

3.

Initialize and Create a PIN: Connect the wallet to your computer or mobile device and follow the on-screen instructions to initialize. You'll be prompted to set up a PIN code, which will protect the device from unauthorized access.

4.

Generate and Record Your Recovery Seed: The device will generate a recovery seed—write down these words on the provided recovery card and keep it in a safe, secure, and separate location. This seed is your lifeline in recovering your wallet should it be lost or damaged.

5.

Install Companion Software: Download and install the official software or app associated with your hardware wallet. This software facilitates interaction with the device, including account management and transaction execution.

6. **Transfer Funds**: Finally, transfer your cryptocurrency funds to the wallet's address. Use the companion software to confirm that the assets have been successfully moved.

At first glance, #### Operating and Transacting with Your Hardware Wallet

Once set up, using a hardware wallet is a straightforward process. Here's how to navigate some common operations:

Performing Transactions: When executing a transaction, connect your hardware wallet to your device, open the companion software, and initiate the transfer.

Verify transaction details on the wallet's screen and authorize it by pressing the confirmation button on the device.

Believe it or not, **Regular Updates**: Keep your hardware wallet firmware and companion software updated to benefit from the latest security measures and additional features.

Manufacturers periodically release updates, which should not be overlooked.

Safe Storage and Handling: Treat your hardware wallet with the same caution as you would other valuable items.

Store it in a dry, secure location, and ensure that your recovery seed is not accessible to others.

Conclusion

Believe it or not, Hardware wallets embody a perfect blend of security and convenience, providing a formidable defense against the myriad threats that lurk in the digital realm.

By incorporating these devices into your cryptocurrency strategy, you embrace a level of protection that instills confidence and peace of mind. As you navigate the complexities of crypto storage, let hardware wallets serve as your unwavering sentinel, standing guard over your digital assets amid an ever-evolving landscape.

Chapter 7: Paper and Brain Wallets: The Art of Minimalist Storage

In an era defined by rapid technological advancement, where digital transactions reign supreme, the desire for simplicity and security persists.

Paper and brain wallets offer a fascinating intersection of minimalism and cryptographic security, providing a compelling approach to cryptocurrency storage. Though not without their challenges, these methods appeal to those who wish to reduce reliance on third-party digital solutions while retaining full control over their assets.

Paper Wallets: Tangible Security

As strange as it sounds, At its core, a paper wallet is a physical document that contains your cryptocurrency public address and its corresponding private key.

This method provides a unique form of offline storage, often referred to as "cold storage," that completely severs the connection between your digital assets and the internet. This isolation drastically reduces exposure to hacking, making it a highly secure option when executed correctly.

Creating a Paper Wallet

To create a paper wallet, visit a reputable online paper wallet generator. Ideally, download the generator to operate it offline, adding an extra layer of security by eliminating exposure to online threats during the process.

A common choice is the open-source project WalletGenerator. net, though due diligence regarding current security practices and potential vulnerabilities is vital.

As strange as it sounds, After generating the wallet, you will receive a pair of keys: the public key (or address) for receiving cryptocurrencies, and the private key for spending them.

Print this information and consider incorporating QR codes for ease of transfers. Secure the physical copy using tools like a laser printer—inkjet printouts may degrade over time—and opt for high-quality materials.

Securing Your Paper Wallet

The unyielding advantage of paper wallets is their immunity to digital theft. However, this method introduces a dependency on physical security.

As a tangible object, the wallet is susceptible to being lost, stolen, or damaged. The responsibility lies entirely with the owner to safeguard this critical piece of paper.

Many people don't realize this, but Store your paper wallet in a secure physical location, such as a safe or a safety deposit box.

Consider laminating the paper to protect against water damage and note the importance of maintaining a backup in a separate location—perhaps even a fireproof safe—in case of unforeseen calamities.

Brain Wallets: Mental Fortresses

For those who wish to embrace an even more minimalist form of security, brain wallets present an alluring solution.

This method involves storing the mnemonic phrase or passphrase associated with your cryptocurrency wallet entirely in your mind. This approach eliminates any physical or digital footprint, relying solely on memory.

Creating a Brain Wallet

The creation of a brain wallet begins with generating a secure passphrase.

This crucial step must balance complexity with memorability—a simple phrase is far too vulnerable to brute force attempts, while an overly complex one risks being forgotten. Consider using a combination of random words or crafting a unique sentence that is both long and unpredictable.

Tools such as the BIP-39 standard can assist in developing such passphrases.

They generate a list of words designed for human memorization yet strong enough to fend off attacks. Opt for a mnemonic phrase with at least 12 words, but remember that 24 words will significantly enhance security.

Securing Your Brain Wallet

The security of a brain wallet relies entirely on the human memory, which introduces unique challenges.

On one hand, it places control solely within the mind—free from physical loss or digital theft. On the other hand, the risk of forgetting or misremembering the phrase poses a significant threat to the recoverability of your assets.

To mitigate the risks, regularly rehearse the mnemonic phrase to reinforce memory retention.

Resist the temptation to store written or digital backups, as this negates the minimalist premise of the brain wallet. Still, keep in mind that the psychological burden of maintaining this form of storage may not suit everyone.

Balancing Minimalism with Practicality

Paper and brain wallets epitomize minimalist storage methods but require a strategic approach to security and practicality.

While paper wallets offer a physical form of cold storage, they demand rigorous attention to safeguarding the material. Brain wallets eliminate physical artifacts but place immense trust in human memory.

To navigate these minimalist methods effectively, consider your personal preferences, lifestyle, and ability to mitigate potential risks.

For instance, while a brain wallet may appeal to a tech-savvy minimalist with a sharp memory, a paper wallet might better suit someone who values the peace of mind provided by a tangible backup.

I've seen this happen before: Remember that neither method is categorically superior; their efficacy hinges on correct implementation and adherence to security best practices.

Regardless of choice, seek a balance between minimalism and security—employing paper or brain wallets as part of a broader strategy that might include other forms of cold or hot storage.

In the evolving landscape of cryptocurrency storage solutions, paper and brain wallets stand out for their distinctive blend of simplicity and security.

Whether you choose to entrust your assets to the durability of paper or the resilience of your memory, these methods reflect a commitment to personal control and secure storage that aligns with the pioneering spirit of the cryptocurrency revolution. As with all things financial, prudence and preparation are the keystones of success—whether stored on paper or in the mind.

Chapter 8: Custodial vs. Non-Custodial Wallets: Know the Difference

In the dynamic world of cryptocurrency, the way you store your assets is as crucial as the way you acquire them.

Understanding the nuances between custodial and non-custodial wallets is paramount to securing your digital wealth. This chapter delves into these two types of wallets, elucidating their respective benefits and risks so that you can make informed decisions about where and how to store your digital assets.

Custodial Wallets: Entrusting Your Crypto to a Third Party

Custodial wallets are akin to traditional banking systems where a financial institution holds and manages assets on behalf of the customer.

In the world of crypto, custodial wallets are provided by third-party services such as exchanges, brokerage platforms, or specialized custodians. By design, custodial wallets take responsibility for safeguarding your private keys, thereby giving you indirect control over your cryptocurrency.

How Custodial Wallets Work

When you create an account on a cryptocurrency exchange or platform, you are usually given a custodial wallet.

The platform holds your private keys and manages the security of your account, allowing you to perform transactions without the need to handle the complex aspects of cryptographic security.

Advantages of Custodial Wallets

1. **User-Friendly**: Custodial wallets are often more accessible for beginners. They offer convenient interfaces and customer support, simplifying transactions and management.

2. **Security Measures**: Large custodial platforms typically implement advanced security measures such as cold storage, multi-signature wallets, and insurance against hacking.

3. **Recovery Options**: If you lose access to your account, the platform often provides recovery options to regain access, such as identity verification processes.

4. **Integrated Services**: Custodial wallets usually come with integrated services like trading, lending, and staking, offering a comprehensive financial ecosystem within one platform.

Risks of Custodial Wallets

At first glance, 1.

Trust: The primary downside is that you must place trust in a third party to manage your private keys. Breaches in their security can lead to loss or theft of your assets.

2. **Regulatory Risks**: Custodial services may be subject to government regulations, leading to potential access issues, account freezes, or sharing of your data with authorities.

3.

Downtime and Withdrawal Limits: Some custodial services can face technical issues or impose withdrawal limits during periods of high demand, hindering access to your funds.

Non-Custodial Wallets: True Ownership

Non-custodial wallets represent the essence of cryptocurrency's original vision: personal sovereignty and control over one's own assets.

These wallets allow users to hold and manage their private keys directly, granting full authority over their crypto assets.

How Non-Custodial Wallets Work

To be honest, When you set up a non-custodial wallet, you are provided with a pair of cryptographic keys: a public key for receiving funds and a private key for signing transactions.

This private key is the linchpin of your wallet's security, and losing it equates to losing access to your assets.

Advantages of Non-Custodial Wallets

1.

Complete Control: Non-custodial wallets grant you full control over your funds. You can transact without intermediaries and are not subject to third-party terms or conditions.

Believe it or not, 2.

Privacy: These wallets enhance privacy, as they do not require users to provide personal information to use the service, insulating you from tracking and third-party scrutiny.

3. **Resistance to Censorship**: Without being tied to a custodian, your funds are less vulnerable to government interference or account freezes.

Risks of Non-Custodial Wallets

1.

Personal Responsibility: The liberty of holding your keys comes with the weight of securing them. If you lose your private key or seed phrase, there is typically no recovery method, resulting in permanent loss of access to your assets.

2. **Technical Complexity**: Non-custodial wallets can be daunting for new users due to their complexity and the responsibility of managing security.

3. **Lack of Integrated Features**: Unlike custodial wallets, these often lack built-in services like exchanges or staking, requiring users to seek these functionalities separately.

Making the Right Choice: Evaluating Your Needs

Choosing between custodial and non-custodial wallets is not simply a technical decision but a reflection of your personal priorities and risk tolerance. Consider these factors:

- **Security versus Convenience**: If you value convenience and are willing to trust a third party, a custodial wallet may be suitable.

However, if you prioritize security and control, a non-custodial solution aligns with those values.

- **Experience Level**: New crypto investors might find custodial wallets less intimidating, while seasoned users with a good grasp of digital security might lean towards non-custodial options.

- **Investment Goals**: For those actively trading or utilizing decentralized finance (DeFi) services, non-custodial wallets are generally preferred to circumvent intermediaries.

Conversely, long-term holders may find the services and protections of custodial wallets more beneficial.

Striking a Balance

It's worth noting that Many investors opt for a hybrid approach, using both types of wallets to diversify their risk.

For instance, keeping a portion of their holdings in a custodial wallet for ease of access and liquidity, while safeguarding the majority in a non-custodial wallet to ensure maximum security and control.

Conclusion: Informed Decisions Safeguard Your Investments

The decision between custodial and non-custodial wallets is not a binary one but rather a spectrum of considerations that includes security, control, convenience, and personal responsibility.

As you delve deeper into the crypto ecosystem, the awareness and knowledge of how these wallets operate will become integral to safeguarding your digital assets. Armed with the insights from this chapter, you are now better equipped to evaluate your needs and choose a strategy that aligns with your risk profile and investment goals, ensuring your crypto journey is both secure and prosperous.

Chapter 9: Setting Up Your First Crypto Wallet: A Step-by-Step Guide

Venturing into the realm of cryptocurrencies can be an exhilarating journey, but it begins with a fundamental step: setting up your first crypto wallet. A wallet serves as the critical interface between you and the crypto-verse, providing the means to store, manage, and transact your digital assets securely.

Understanding how to properly set up a wallet is paramount for anyone looking to delve into the world of digital currencies. This chapter will walk you through the process of selecting, installing, and securing your first crypto wallet with precision and clarity.

1. Choosing the Right Wallet Type

I've seen this happen before: The first decision entails selecting the type of wallet that best suits your needs.

Crypto wallets are broadly categorized into two types: hot wallets (online) and cold wallets (offline).

Hot Wallets: These are digital wallets connected to the internet, suitable for users who need frequent access to their cryptocurrency.

Hot wallets are convenient and come in the form of desktop or mobile applications as well as web-based platforms. Their ease of access makes them an ideal choice for beginners trading or making transactions regularly.

Cold Wallets: These are physical devices or paper wallets not connected to the internet, designed to store cryptocurrencies securely.

Cold wallets are recommended for storing large amounts of crypto over a long period, minimizing the risk of cyber attacks.

For beginners, a hot wallet offers the ideal balance between accessibility and security.

As you further explore cryptocurrencies, you may later integrate a cold wallet for enhanced security.

2. Selecting a Reputable Wallet Provider

With numerous wallet providers available, identifying a reputable service is crucial. When selecting a provider, consider the following factors:

- **Security Features**: Ensure the wallet offers robust security measures, such as two-factor authentication, biometric access, and encryption.

- **User Experience**: A user-friendly interface facilitates easier navigation, crucial for beginners.

- **Reputation and Reviews**: Research the wallet provider's reputation through user reviews and community feedback.

It's worth noting that - **Compatibility**: Confirm that the wallet supports a broad range of cryptocurrencies, particularly those you plan to use.

Some reliable wallet providers include Exodus, Trust Wallet, and MetaMask for hot wallets, and Ledger or Trezor for cold wallets.

Evaluate each according to your personal requirements, preferences, and desired level of security.

3. Installing the Wallet

Believe it or not, After selecting a wallet provider, the installation process begins. Follow these steps for a hot wallet setup on a mobile device:

- **Download the App**: Visit the official website for the wallet provider or use authorized app stores (Google Play Store or Apple App Store) to download the mobile application.

Be wary of fraudulent apps; always verify authenticity through official sources.

Believe it or not, - **Create a New Wallet**: After installing, open the app and select the option to create a new wallet.

This step generates a new wallet address and private keys unique to your account.

- **Set a Strong Password**: Choose a complex, unique password.

Avoid easily guessed patterns or repetitions. This is an imperative layer of security to your account.

- **Back-Up Your Seed Phrase**: The seed phrase, or recovery phrase, is a sequence of words that backs up your wallet.

Write it down on paper and store it securely. Avoid digital storage methods such as taking screenshots, due to their vulnerability.

4. Securing Your Wallet

At first glance, Security is paramount in the crypto world. Successfully managing your wallet involves adopting best practices to safeguard your assets:

- **Enable Two-Factor Authentication (2FA)**: Enhance your wallet's security by enabling 2FA.

This adds an extra layer of verification, typically through a code sent to your mobile device.

At first glance, - **Stay Updated**: Regularly update your wallet application to protect against security vulnerabilities. Updates often include critical patches and security improvements.

- **Beware of Phishing Attacks**: Phishing attacks are a prevalent threat in the crypto space, where malicious actors attempt to deceive you into revealing your private keys or personal information.

Be cautious with communications that appear unsolicited or require urgent action, and never disclose your seed phrase to anyone.

- **Regularly Review Activity**: Maintain vigilance by regularly reviewing your wallet activity for unauthorized transactions or anomalies.

Taking swift action at the first sign of irregularity can prevent potential loss.

5. Receiving and Sending Cryptocurrencies

Let's not forget, With your wallet set up and secured, you can now send and receive cryptocurrencies:

- **Receiving Crypto**: Locate your wallet's unique receiving address, typically found under the 'Receive' tab or option.

To receive funds, provide the sender with this specific address. Always double-check the address before sharing it.

- **Sending Crypto**: To send funds, navigate to the 'Send' tab in your wallet, input the recipient's wallet address, specify the amount to transfer, and confirm the transaction.

Pay attention to network fees, which fluctuate depending on network congestion.

6. Maintaining Regular Safeguarding Practices

Lastly, establishing regular practices to maintain your wallet's security is vital:

- **Periodic Back-Ups**: Ensure that your seed phrase is backed up at multiple secure locations.

Periodic back-ups protect against unforeseen circumstances, such as loss or damage to your original storage.

- **Informative Awareness**: Stay informed on the latest security threats and techniques within the crypto ecosystem.

Engage with trusted sources of information and forums for the latest updates.

By now, you will have successfully navigated the essential steps to set up and secure your first cryptocurrency wallet.

Remember, the cornerstone of your journey in the cryptocurrency landscape is securely managing your digital assets. As you continue to explore and interact with the dynamic and transformative world of crypto, employing these foundational practices will safeguard your assets against potential risks, empowering you to trade and invest with confidence.

Chapter 10: Best Practices for Backing Up Your Wallet

In the digital realm where cryptocurrencies reside, your wallet's security is paramount. A cornerstone of this security is effectively backing up your wallet.

While the notion of backing up may seem simple, ensuring it is done correctly is anything but trivial. This chapter will guide you through industry-standard practices and innovative techniques to secure your digital assets unequivocally.

Understanding the Importance of a Backup

It's worth noting that A backup, in essence, is a safeguard—a lifeline in scenarios where your primary access to cryptocurrency falters. Whether it's due to hardware failures, software glitches, or human error, a backup ensures continuous access to your assets.

Losing your wallet without a backup is akin to losing physical cash on the street, with no hope of recovery. Unlike traditional banking systems, cryptocurrencies operate on absolute control, meaning the holder of the wallet is the sole proprietor of its contents. Thus, a robust backup strategy is essential.

The Anatomy of a Backup

When backing up your cryptocurrency wallet, there are several elements to consider:

It's worth noting that 1. **Seed Phrase**: This is a series of words generated by your wallet that grants access to your cryptocurrency.

The seed phrase is often 12 to 24 words long and represents the private keys for your wallets. It is the most critical element to backup securely.

2. **Private Keys**: Although many modern wallets operate through seed phrases, certain wallets and cryptocurrencies might still use private keys, requiring separate backups.

3. **Wallet Databases**: For some desktop and mobile wallets, a backup of the entire wallet file, which includes transaction history and metadata, might be necessary.

Believe it or not, 4.

Password Authentication: While not a backup in the strictest sense, ensuring that you separately record wallet passwords is crucial for accessing wallet apps that use additional authentication layers.

Optimal Backup Practices

1. **Physical Backup Copies**

Creating physical copies of your seed phrase or private keys is fundamental.

Consider using the following methods:

- **Paper Backup**: Write the seed phrase or private keys by hand on paper.

Store this paper in a safe location, such as a fireproof and waterproof safe. Ensure you have multiple copies stored in different secure locations to mitigate the risk of a localized disaster destroying your only backup.

- **Metal Backup Plates**: For enhanced durability, consider engraving your seed phrase onto a metal plate.

These plates are resistant to fire, water, and physical deterioration over time, offering superior protection for long-term storage.

2. **Digital Backup Strategies**

While paper and metal backups are reliable, integrating digital backups can offer redundancy. However, these should be approached with caution due to potential security vulnerabilities:

- **Encrypted USB Drives**: Store a digital copy of your seed phrase on a USB drive that is encrypted.

This provides an additional layer of security against digital threats. Ensure the encryption password is complex and stored separately, using a password manager if necessary.

Many people don't realize this, but - **Secure Cloud Storage**: Storing your backup in a secure, encrypted cloud service can be convenient, especially for global access.

It's vital to use end-to-end encryption to protect your data from breaches.

3. **Distributed Backups**

A cutting-edge approach is to use Shamir's Secret Sharing, a cryptographic algorithm that splits your seed phrase into multiple parts, requiring a minimum number of parts to reconstruct the original phrase.

This means no single piece contains the full information, offering increased security if some parts are compromised. Distribute these parts across secure locations or with trusted associates.

Security Considerations

A backup strategy is only as strong as its weakest link. Ensure the following to maintain the integrity of your backups:

- **Avoid Online Exposure**: Never store unencrypted backups online or in devices frequently connected to the internet. This minimizes exposure to hacking and malware.

To be honest, - **Trust No One**: Limit who knows about your backups.

The fewer people aware, the lower the risk of human error or malicious intent threatening your assets.

- **Regular Updates**: Consistently review and update your backup methods, especially after any significant wallet activity or change in asset holdings.

Testing Your Backups

At first glance, To prevent unpleasant surprises, periodically test your backups.

Ensure you can successfully restore your wallet from the backup at least once. Testing confirms that your backup method is functioning and that the necessary details are recorded accurately.

Conclusion

Backing up your cryptocurrency wallet with precision is an exercise in both patience and diligence. The methods, while varied, converge on a single aim: the uninterrupted accessibility and security of your cryptocurrency.

By implementing diversified and strategic backup practices, you minimize risk and arm yourself with confidence in this volatile digital world. Like any fortress, the strength of your crypto wallet's security is contingent upon the soundness of its foundation; make your backup strategy part of that unwavering base.

Chapter 11: Key Management: Safeguarding Your Private Keys

In the realm of cryptocurrencies, private keys are often regarded as the keys to the kingdom. They are the cryptographic linchpins that allow you access to your digital assets, enabling the initiation of transactions and the management of your holdings.

Understanding the importance of effectively managing these private keys can make the difference between confidently navigating the world of crypto and falling victim to costly errors or nefarious actors. This chapter unveils the critical aspects of key management, offering you the knowledge needed to safeguard your private keys with the vigilance and precision of a practiced custodian.

The Importance of Private Keys

To truly appreciate the gravitas of private keys, it's imperative to comprehend their foundational role in the cryptocurrency ecosystem. Unlike traditional banking systems, cryptocurrencies are decentralized. This means there is no central authority that holds or can restore access to your funds should you lose your keys.

Private keys are integral to the cryptographic operations that secure the blockchain network. When you own a cryptocurrency, what you possess is a private key—a unique alphanumeric string that gives you exclusive access to your digital assets. Without this key, your funds are irretrievably lost.

Generating Private Keys

Keys can be generated through software wallets, hardware wallets, or sometimes manually by individuals with more technical expertise. To ensure security from the onset, it's essential that key generation is conducted offline in a secure environment.

This eliminates the risk of interception by malware or malicious actors. Hardware wallets are particularly adept at generating keys securely; they use a random number generator to create keys offline, ensuring a high level of security.

Storing Private Keys

Once securely generated, private keys must be stored with the utmost care.

Their security is paramount, as access to these keys equates to ownership of the assets they protect. Storing private keys falls into two broad categories: hot storage and cold storage.

Hot Storage

Interestingly enough, Hot storage refers to keys stored on internet-connected devices. While convenient for frequent trading or transactions, they are inherently at risk of online threats such as hacking, phishing, or malware.

Hot wallets, commonly used for this type of storage, include mobile, desktop, and web wallets. These should only house a small portion of your portfolio, akin to carrying cash for everyday transactions. It's crucial to implement additional security measures such as two-factor authentication and regular software updates to mitigate risk.

Cold Storage

Cold storage offers a more secure solution by keeping keys off the web. This form of storage is ideal for long-term holding and is akin to safeguarding valuables in a vault.

Cold wallets include hardware wallets, paper wallets, and air-gapped computers—devices that have never been and will never be connected to the internet. Hardware wallets are a popular cold storage option; they are typically small, USB-like devices that store keys securely offline while facilitating transactions when connected to a computer with installed security software.

Believe it or not, A paper wallet involves printing your keys and storing them in a safe location. It's critical to ensure that the printer used is not connected to the internet to prevent interception.

Keep the paper wallet in a safe, waterproof, and fire-resistant place. Remember, any damage to or loss of this paper could mean a permanent loss of access to your assets.

Backing Up Your Keys

Accidental deletion, loss, or destruction of private keys equates to loss of access to your cryptocurrency, making backup a crucial step in key management. Always have multiple physical backups of your keys stored in separate secure locations.

These could be in the form of paper wallets, encrypted USB drives, or other secure digital formats that you can retrieve when necessary. Regularly update these backups to reflect any key changes from active use.

Encrypting Your Private Keys

Encryption provides an additional layer of defense by encoding your keys in such a way that only authorized parties can access them. Many hardware and software wallets offer key encryption features, and it's advisable to utilize them.

If keys are backed up digitally, such as in cloud storage, they must be encrypted. Select strong, unique passwords and change them periodically. The use of a password manager, while convenient, should be treated with caution—ensure that it is highly secure and never store your password in plain text.

Mitigating Key Vulnerabilities

As strange as it sounds, Humans are often the weakest link in the security chain. Social engineering and phishing attacks exploit our propensity to trust and can result in lost keys or unauthorized transactions.

Educate yourself continuously on the evolving tactics used by cybercriminals. Stay suspicious of unsolicited communication and avoid sharing your keys in emails or on public platforms. Deploy reputable security software, regularly update your devices, and practice vigilant online behavior.

Preparing for Missteps

Despite best efforts, errors can happen. Forces beyond our control, such as hacking or natural disasters, may compromise key security.

Develop a recovery plan detailing steps to take in the event of key loss or compromise. This should include having reliable contacts—trusted individuals or services—that can assist in recovering funds where possible.

Inheritance Planning

Consider the legacy of your digital assets in the event of your untimely demise. Develop an inheritance plan that includes instructions and secure access to your private keys for your heirs.

This reduces the risk of funds becoming inaccessible upon your passing. Legal frameworks around digital assets are still evolving, so consulting with an estate attorney familiar with cryptocurrency is beneficial.

Conclusion

Let's not forget, The management of private keys is a responsibility that cannot be overstated. As the sole barrier between your assets and potential loss or theft, maintaining the integrity and security of these keys demands diligence, foresight, and continual education.

The strategies delineated in this chapter aim to empower you to wield your keys with confidence and competence. As you delve deeper into the cryptocurrency world, your proficiency in key management will serve as both shield and sword, safeguarding your investments and fortifying your position in this dynamic landscape.

Chapter 12: Wallet Security: Passwords, Passphrases, and 2FA

In the ever-evolving world of cryptocurrency, securing your digital assets is paramount. A breach in your wallet's defenses could result in significant financial loss, especially considering the irreversible nature of blockchain transactions.

Understanding how to implement robust security measures like passwords, passphrases, and two-factor authentication (2FA) is crucial. In this chapter, we delve into these security components, guiding you on how to effectively use them to fortify your crypto assets against potential threats.

The Foundation: Passwords

Many people don't realize this, but Passwords are often your first line of defense against unauthorized access. They must be strong, unique, and not easily guessable. The downfall of many unfortunate crypto holders has been the use of weak or commonly used passwords like "123456" or "password.

" To create a robust password, consider implementing a combination of upper and lower case letters, numbers, and special characters. For instance, a password such as "G8v!ne2$0r7@l" is significantly more secure than "password123. ".

Best Practices for Password Security

1.

Length Matters: Aim for passwords that are at least 12-16 characters long. The longer your password, the harder it is for hackers to crack it using brute force attacks.

To be honest, 2. **Avoid Repetition:** Never reuse passwords across different platforms. If one account is compromised, others remain secure.

3.

Randomness is Key: Use password managers to generate and store random passwords. Tools like LastPass, Bitwarden, or 1Password can help maintain complex passwords without the need to memorize them all.

4. **Regular Updates:** Change your passwords regularly. Set a calendar reminder to update them every three to six months.

The Next Level: Passphrases

While strong passwords are crucial, passphrases offer an enhanced layer of security.

A passphrase is a sequence of words or a sentence that is easy for you to remember but difficult for others to guess. Unlike traditional passwords, which can be cryptic, passphrases can be more intuitive, making them an excellent option for securing your crypto wallet.

Crafting Secure Passphrases

Interestingly enough, 1.

Use Multiple Words: A passphrase should consist of four or more random words that create a mental picture or story. For example, "BlueMonkeySailsChocolate" is both memorable and secure.

2. **Incorporate Variation:** Mix in numbers or special characters. A passphrase like "BlueMonkey@123%SailsChocolate" increases complexity without sacrificing memorability.

3. **Avoid Common Phrases:** Steer clear of famous quotations or song lyrics, as these are often part of password-cracking databases.

Many people don't realize this, but 4.

Test Memorability: Ensure you can recall the passphrase without assistance. Write it down on paper and store it securely until memorized, then destroy the paper.

Reinforcing Defenses: Two-Factor Authentication (2FA)

Two-factor authentication (2FA) adds a critical layer of security by requiring a secondary piece of information beyond your password or passphrase.

Even if a hacker obtains your password, 2FA makes it significantly more challenging for them to gain access to your account.

Implementing 2FA Effectively

1.

Choose an Authenticator App: Use an authenticator app like Google Authenticator, Authy, or Microsoft Authenticator instead of relying on SMS 2FA. These apps generate time-sensitive codes that are more secure and less vulnerable to interception.

2.

Backup Authentication Codes: Some accounts provide backup codes during the 2FA setup process. Store these codes securely, as they can be crucial for account recovery if you lose access to your authentication device.

In real life, 3.

Stay Alert to Phishing Attacks: Ensure that any 2FA requests are legitimate, as phishing attempts often mimic authentication processes to steal your credentials.

4. **Regular Review and Update:** Periodically review your 2FA settings and update them if you switch devices or lose access to your current authenticator app.

Synergizing Security Measures

It's worth noting that An effective wallet security strategy involves combining robust passwords, well-crafted passphrases, and diligent use of 2FA.

Here's how you can synergize these elements for maximal protection:.

- **Use a Password Manager:** Store all your complex passwords securely, while your wallet can be secured with a formidable passphrase.

- **Enable 2FA on All Accounts:** Not just your crypto wallets, but also your email and any service that supports this feature.

Often, failure to secure secondary accounts can lead to breaches.

- **Educate Yourself Continually:** Cyber threats evolve, so your knowledge and understanding of security must also evolve. Regularly update yourself on the latest security tactics.

- **Practice Digital Hygiene:** Regularly clear cookies, update software, and ensure your devices are protected by antivirus programs.

Recovering from a Security Breach

As strange as it sounds, Even with all precautions, breaches can occur.

Knowing how to respond swiftly can minimize potential losses. Should you suspect unauthorized access, act immediately by:.

- **Changing Passwords/Passphrases:** Re-secure your accounts by altering all known credentials.

- **Reassessing 2FA Configurations:** Ensure your 2FA settings have not been tampered with and update them as necessary.

At first glance, - **Monitoring Accounts Diligently:** Observe for any unusual transactions or activities and report them to affected platforms.

- **Contacting Relevant Authorities:** Reach out to the platforms for support and consider reporting significant breaches to cybersecurity authorities for broader protective measures.

In conclusion, securing your cryptocurrency wallet is a multi-faceted endeavor that requires vigilance, careful planning, and continual updates to your security practices.

The integration of strong passwords, thoughtful passphrases, and robust two-factor authentication is not just recommended, it is necessary to safeguard your digital assets in an increasingly uncertain cyber landscape. By implementing these measures, you are not merely relying on hope, but building a fortress around your valuable crypto holdings.

Chapter 13: Phishing, Scams, and Social Engineering in Crypto

The cryptocurrency revolution has undeniably transformed the financial landscape, introducing new paradigms of decentralization, privacy, and cross-border transactions. However, with these innovations come challenges, particularly in the realm of security.

Among these threats, phishing, scams, and social engineering stand out as prevalent and persistent dangers that can compromise your crypto holdings if not diligently guarded against. To navigate the cryptosphere like a pro, it's imperative to understand these threats in detail and adopt robust strategies to safeguard your assets.

Understanding Phishing in Crypto

Believe it or not, Phishing is a form of cyberattack that tricks individuals into divulging confidential information, such as private keys or login credentials.

In the crypto world, phishing attacks are often disguised as legitimate communications from exchanges, wallet providers, or even well-known industry figures. These fraudulent messages typically come via email, social media, or messaging apps, often urging immediate action by creating a sense of urgency.

For instance, you might receive an email appearing to be from your cryptocurrency exchange, warning you of suspicious login attempts and prompting you to verify your account by clicking a link.

This link redirects you to a fake website that closely mimics the original, designed to capture your login details. Once the attacker has your credentials, your cryptocurrency holdings can be swiftly siphoned away.

Key signs of phishing include:

- Unexpected messages from exchanges or wallet services.

- Urgent language prompting immediate action.

- Suspicious URLs or email addresses that deviate slightly from legitimate ones.

- Requests for personal information.

To protect against phishing, it's essential to always verify the authenticity of communications.

Hover over links to check their real destination, and cross-reference any unexpected messages directly with the service provider using known contact methods.

Navigating Crypto Scams

Crypto scams take on various forms, evolving constantly to exploit unsuspecting investors.

From fake initial coin offerings (ICOs) to Ponzi schemes and fraudulent exchanges, the ingenuity of scammers knows no bounds.

A classic example is the fake ICO, where scammers create a seemingly legitimate coin offering to attract investments.

These offerings often promise unrealistic returns, leveraging slick marketing materials and fabricated testimonials. Once investment goals are met, the fraudsters disappear with the funds, leaving investors empty-handed.

Believe it or not, To avoid falling prey to scams, diligent research is your best ally. Verify project legitimacy by:

- Exploring the team credentials and their reputations in the industry.

- Assessing the utility and demand for the proposed project.

I've seen this happen before: - Reviewing the whitepaper to ensure it presents a viable and coherent business plan.

- Checking for endorsements from reputable figures or organizations in the crypto space.

Similarly, be cautious of schemes promising guaranteed returns or those requiring upfront payments for rewards.

If it sounds too good to be true, it likely is.

Social Engineering: The Human Factor

Social engineering exploits the weakest link in the security chain: humans.

Crypto social engineering attacks are insidious and can take many forms, preying on individuals' trust, fears, or ignorance.

Many people don't realize this, but Consider a scenario where an attacker impersonates a trusted figure in the crypto community, initiating a conversation through social media.

Over time, they build rapport, eventually soliciting sensitive information under the guise of assistance or collaboration.

Attackers may also pose as support staff from crypto exchanges or wallets, reaching out proactively to 'solve' a problem you weren't even aware of.

By cleverly manipulating situations, they gain access to accounts, often without the target realizing until it's too late.

Fend off social engineering attempts by practicing vigilance:

- Be skeptical of unsolicited communications from individuals claiming to represent official entities.

It's worth noting that - Avoid sharing sensitive information through unsecured or unfamiliar channels.

- Enable two-factor authentication (2FA) on accounts to add an extra layer of security.

- Trust, but verify every interaction, especially those involving financial transactions.

Building a Fortress: Your Defense Strategy

Interestingly enough, Creating a comprehensive defense strategy against these threats involves layered security and continuous education. Here's how you can fortify your crypto holdings:

1.

Educate Yourself Continuously: Stay informed about the latest tactics used by phishers and scammers. Engage with trusted crypto communities and news sources to keep abreast of emerging threats.

2.

Deploy Strong Authentication: Use complex passwords and change them regularly. Activate 2FA on all crypto-related accounts where possible, opting for app-based authentication over SMS for enhanced security.

At first glance, 3.

Secure Your Devices: Ensure that all devices used to access cryptocurrency are secure, with up-to-date anti-virus software, operating systems, and firewalls. Regularly back up your wallet data offline.

4.

Maintain Operational OpSec: Practice operational security by minimizing the personal information you share online. This includes refraining from announcing crypto holdings publicly and being conscious of how much is revealed on social media.

5.

Evaluate Transactions Meticulously: Double-check wallet addresses for accuracy before sending transactions, and confirm all transaction details. Use a small test transaction for significant transfers to verify recipient integrity.

To be honest, 6.

Rely on Cold Storage: Whenever feasible, store the majority of your crypto assets in cold wallets, which are less susceptible to online attacks.

7. **Foster a Security Mindset**: Develop a culture of security awareness within yourself and your family, recognizing that the threat landscape is ever-evolving.

While the promise of cryptocurrency is enticing, remaining vigilant and informed is vital to keeping your assets safe from malicious actors.

By understanding phishing, scams, and social engineering in the crypto world, you are better equipped to navigate this dynamic landscape confidently and securely. The battle against cybercrime in crypto is ongoing, but with the right knowledge and tools, you can ensure that your wallets remain secure, allowing you to engage in the crypto revolution with peace of mind.

Chapter 14: Cross-Platform Wallets: Handling Multiple Cryptocurrencies

In the rapidly evolving world of cryptocurrency, the need for managing various digital assets efficiently is more pressing than ever.

As cryptocurrencies gain mainstream attention, a diverse user base is looking for solutions that cater to different coins without compromising security or usability. Enter cross-platform wallets—a crucial tool for anyone serious about managing multiple cryptocurrencies seamlessly.

Understanding Cross-Platform Wallets

Cross-platform wallets are digital wallets that support various cryptocurrencies within a single interface.

Unlike single-currency wallets, which are optimized for a singular type of cryptocurrency, cross-platform wallets offer versatility, supporting multiple blockchain protocols and asset types. This functionality appeals to both seasoned traders who frequently dabble in different cryptocurrencies and newcomers who seek a straightforward approach to managing diverse digital investments.

Primary benefits of cross-platform wallets include reduced complexity, cost savings, and convenience.

By allowing the user to store, send, and receive multiple types of cryptocurrencies in one location, these wallets eliminate the need for numerous accounts with different wallet providers.

Beyond mere storage, cross-platform wallets often offer additional features like in-app exchanges, staking rewards for certain coins, portfolio tracking, and sometimes even debit card integrations.

These features are particularly appealing for users seeking a comprehensive platform for all their cryptocurrency needs.

Types of Cross-Platform Wallets

Cross-platform wallets typically come in two forms: software wallets and hardware wallets. Each has its unique features and security considerations.

Software Wallets

Software wallets are applications or programs installed on your mobile device, desktop, or accessed through a web browser. These are often preferred for their accessibility and ease-of-use.

Well-known examples include Exodus, Trust Wallet, and Atomic Wallet. They provide a user-friendly interface that supports a wide array of cryptocurrencies.

Security is a major concern with software wallets, given their vulnerability to malware and other online threats.

Nonetheless, many have integrated robust security features such as biometric authentication, two-factor authentication (2FA), and multi-signature support to enhance safety.

Another advantage of software wallets is their capacity to facilitate direct trading between supported currencies.

This feature, often called atomic swaps, allows users to exchange cryptocurrencies without involving third-party exchanges, reducing transaction fees and counterparty risk.

Hardware Wallets

For those who prioritize security above all else, hardware wallets can be an ideal choice.

These physical devices store your cryptocurrency offline, which helps protect against hacks and malware that often target software wallets. Some popular multi-currency hardware wallets include Ledger and Trezor.

While hardware wallets are less convenient for fast transactions compared to their software counterparts, they excel in secure long-term storage.

They support a wide range of cryptocurrencies, albeit usually necessitating a connection to a software interface for sending and receiving funds. The balance of security and compatibility makes hardware wallets a favorite among serious investors holding a diverse portfolio.

Key Features to Look For

When choosing a cross-platform wallet, several aspects demand careful consideration.

1. **Security:** The primary concern should always be security. Opt for wallets with strong encryption standards, reliable authentication processes, and active security audits.

As strange as it sounds, 2.

User Experience: A user-friendly interface can significantly impact your experience. Look for wallets with simple setup processes and intuitive navigation.

3. **Coin Compatibility:** Ensure that the wallet supports the cryptocurrencies you own.

As blockchain projects proliferate, new coins and tokens continue to emerge. Select a wallet that updates frequently to support new additions.

4. **Integration and Functionality:** Features like integrated exchanges, DeFi support, and blockchain interoperability can enhance your use of a cross-platform wallet.

Believe it or not, 5.

Community and Support: A strong community presence and reliable customer support can prove invaluable, especially when navigating issues or learning how to best utilize wallet features.

Best Practices for Managing Cross-Platform Wallets

Using cross-platform wallets efficiently requires adherence to best practices, which ensure both security and fluid operation across various currencies.

I've seen this happen before: - **Backup Your Seed Phrase:** Seed phrases are a critical component of any wallet for recovery purposes.

Store them securely in offline locations to recover your wallet if you lose your device or forget your password.

- **Enable Multi-layer Security Features:** Make use of all available security options—biometric login, 2FA, and multi-signature authorization. Each additional layer boosts your wallet's security.

- **Regular Updates:** Keep your wallet and its security features up-to-date. Regular updates often include patches for newly discovered vulnerabilities.

In real life, - **Separate Hot and Cold Storage:** Use hardware wallets or other secure offline methods for storing significant quantities long-term, while employing software wallets for smaller, everyday transactions.

- **Stay Informed:** The crypto world is dynamic and subject to rapid changes.

Keep abreast of the latest developments affecting your wallet provider or the currencies you manage within it.

Conclusion

Cross-platform wallets are indispensable tools for managing a diverse portfolio of cryptocurrencies.

They provide not only convenience but also advanced features that can enhance both your security and trading experience.

When chosen with care and used responsibly, these wallets can simplify the often-complicated landscape of digital asset management.

By understanding their intricacies and aligning your choice with your unique needs, you can harness the full potential of cross-platform wallets and handle multiple cryptocurrencies like a professional.

Chapter 15: Integrating Wallets with Decentralized Applications (dApps)

In the evolving landscape of blockchain technology, decentralized applications, or dApps, represent a significant leap towards a decentralized future. These applications offer increased security, transparency, and autonomy, drawing enthusiasts and developers alike.

However, to interact effectively with dApps, a fundamental component is the integration with cryptocurrency wallets. This chapter aims to unravel the process, intricacies, and strategies involved in integrating wallets with dApps, empowering you to leverage these applications securely and effectively.

Understanding dApps: The Decentralized Paradigm

Before delving into the technicalities of wallet integration, it is necessary to comprehend the foundational structure of dApps.

Unlike traditional applications, which rely on centralized servers, dApps operate on decentralized networks, typically utilizing blockchain technology. This decentralized architecture provides enhanced security features due to its immutability and distribution across numerous nodes, eliminating single points of failure.

dApps can be categorized based on their utility and scope—ranging from financial platforms in decentralized finance (DeFi) to blockchain-based games, supply chain management, and beyond.

As use cases expand, the need for seamless wallet integration becomes imperative, allowing users to interact with these platforms smoothly and securely.

The Role of Cryptocurrency Wallets

It's worth noting that Cryptocurrency wallets act as the gateway through which users access the blockchain ecosystem, including dApps.

These wallets are essential for managing your digital assets, confirming transactions, and accessing decentralized platforms. Wallets can be broadly categorized into software wallets, hardware wallets, and paper wallets, each with its unique advantages and trade-offs.

Software Wallets: These are applications or browser extensions that store private keys online.

They are user-friendly and integrate seamlessly with dApps, making them a popular choice for frequent transactions. MetaMask is a prime example, often used as a bridge to the Ethereum blockchain and its myriad of dApps.

Hardware Wallets: These are physical devices designed to store private keys offline, hence offering superior security against online threats.

While integrating hardware wallets with dApps may involve additional steps, they are indispensable for storing large amounts of crypto assets securely.

Believe it or not, **Paper Wallets**: Although less common for dApp interaction, paper wallets consist of physical documents containing private keys.

As they do not integrate directly with dApps, users must first import the keys into a software wallet.

Steps to Integrate Wallets with dApps

Integrating a wallet with a dApp is generally a straightforward process, especially with the majority of wallets designed to support such operations.

Here's a step-by-step guide to ensure a secure and efficient integration:.

Step 1: Select a Suitable Wallet

Choosing the right wallet depends on your specific needs.

For users frequently interacting with dApps, a software wallet like MetaMask or Trust Wallet provides ease of use and direct compatibility. If security is your priority, consider hardware wallets such as Ledger or Trezor, but be prepared for a slightly more involved setup when engaging with dApps.

Step 2: Install and Configure the Wallet

For software wallets:

1. Download the wallet application or install the browser extension from a trusted source.

2. Create a new wallet, following the setup instructions.

As strange as it sounds, 3. Safely store your seed phrase—a critical step in ensuring recovery in case of loss or damage.

For hardware wallets:

It's worth noting that 1. Set up the device following the manufacturer's guidelines.

2. Connect the hardware wallet to the computer when interacting with compatible software applications or extensions.

Step 3: Connect the Wallet to a dApp

Once your wallet is configured:

To be honest, 1. Navigate to the dApp you wish to interact with.

2. Look for a "Connect Wallet" option – this is typically located in the top right corner of the dApp's interface.

3. Select your wallet from the list of options. For instance, selecting "MetaMask" if you are using its extension.

Step 4: Authorize the Connection

As strange as it sounds, When prompted, authorize the dApp to access your wallet.

Ensure this is a trusted dApp to prevent malicious interactions. Most wallets will display a confirmation screen where you can verify the dApp's URL and your account details before granting access.

Step 5: Conduct Transactions

With the wallet connected, you can now perform transactions, participate in staking, lend assets, or whatever functionality the dApp offers.

Each transaction will require your confirmation, allowing you to review its details, fees, and implications before proceeding.

Best Practices for Security

While integrating wallets with dApps offers incredible convenience and powerful functionalities, it also exposes you to risks if proper precautions are not taken.

Here are best practices to guard your assets:.

- **Verify dApp Authenticity**: Prioritize the use of reputable dApps and scrutinize URLs to avoid phishing sites that mimic legitimate platforms.

- **Regularly Monitor Permissions**: Periodically review and manage the permissions granted to dApps within your wallet, revoking access from those no longer in use.

In real life, - **Security Updates**: Keep your wallet and any related extensions updated to benefit from security patches and enhancements.

- **Hardware Wallet Utilization**: Use hardware wallets for significant transactions, providing an additional security layer by storing your keys offline.

The Future of Wallet-dApp Integration

As blockchain technology evolves, so do the mechanisms underpinning wallet and dApp integration.

Expect innovations geared toward enhancing user convenience without compromising on security. Cross-chain compatibility, improved user interfaces, and advanced security protocols are likely to shape the next generation of wallet-dApp integration, fostering greater adoption and trust in decentralized applications.

In conclusion, mastering the integration of wallets with dApps is an essential skill set for anyone venturing into the world of blockchain.

By choosing the right tools, understanding the integration process, and adhering to security best practices, you can confidently navigate this dynamic ecosystem, unlocking the full potential of decentralized applications with efficiency and security.

Chapter 16: Navigating Crypto Wallet Exchanges: Pros and Cons

Cryptocurrency wallets are a fundamental component of the blockchain ecosystem, allowing users to store, send, and receive digital assets. However, not all wallets are created equal.

Among the various types, exchange-based wallets are a popular choice for many users due to their convenience and integrated services. In this chapter, we will dissect the intricacies of crypto wallet exchanges, examining their advantages, drawbacks, and whether they align with your crypto management strategy.

What are Crypto Wallet Exchanges?

I've seen this happen before: Crypto wallet exchanges are platforms that not only facilitate the trading of cryptocurrencies but also provide integrated wallet services for storing digital assets.

When you sign up for a crypto exchange like Coinbase, Binance, or Kraken, you essentially get a custodial wallet that holds your cryptocurrencies for you. These wallets are part of the platform's infrastructure, enabling seamless trading and transfers without the need for additional transactions between separate wallets.

The Pros of Using Exchange-Based Wallets

1. **User-Friendly Interface**: One of the main appeals of exchange-based wallets is their intuitive design.

They are tailored for the average user, allowing for easy navigation whether you're a seasoned trader or a newcomer to the crypto world. Exchanges often provide comprehensive dashboards that offer a clear overview of your portfolio, market trends, and transaction history, making them an excellent choice for users who prefer simplicity.

Believe it or not, 2. **Integrated Trading Facilities**: A prime advantage of using exchange wallets is their seamless integration with trading functions.

With everything in one place, you can quickly execute trades without the hassle of sending assets across different platforms. This integration not only speeds up transactions but also reduces fees associated with cross-platform transfers.

3. **Access to a Wide Range of Cryptocurrencies**: Exchange wallets provide access to a broad array of cryptocurrencies.

Most leading exchanges list hundreds of coins and tokens, far more than you could feasibly manage across individual wallets. This broad access can be particularly beneficial for traders looking to diversify their portfolios or explore lesser-known assets.

4.

Security Features: Beyond ease of use, many exchanges prioritize security. While it's true custodial wallets inherently mean surrendering some control, exchanges invest heavily in robust security protocols, including two-factor authentication, withdrawal whitelist, and cold storage mechanisms, which keep a considerable portion of user funds offline to mitigate risks of hacking.

Interestingly enough, 5. **Liquidity**: Exchanges are unmatched when it comes to liquidity.

High trading volumes on popular platforms ensure that you can buy and sell crypto assets quickly at market value. This liquidity is crucial for active traders looking to capitalize on market movements.

The Cons of Using Exchange-Based Wallets

1. **Custodial Control**: Perhaps the most significant downside of exchange wallets is that they are custodial by design.

This means you do not have full control over your private keys—essentially, your crypto assets are in the hands of the exchange. In the event of a hack or the insolvency of the exchange, you stand the risk of losing your assets.

Interestingly enough, 2. **Potential for Hacks**: Despite rigorous security measures, exchanges remain prime targets for cyberattacks.

The history of cryptocurrency is rife with examples where exchanges have suffered breaches, resulting in substantial losses of user funds. While insurance and reimbursement plans are often in place, the risk remains significant.

3. **Regulatory Risks**: As centralized entities, exchanges are subject to regulations that can change abruptly.

Regulatory actions can sometimes affect your ability to access your funds or influence the transaction fees and services available to you. The pseudonymous nature of cryptocurrency transactions further compounds these regulatory issues.

4. **Limited Privacy**: When using company-managed exchange wallets, users must comply with know-your-customer (KYC) procedures.

While this brings about certain protections, such as regulatory compliance and fraud prevention, it affects the anonymity of your transactions. Privacy-focused individuals might find this requirement unappealing.

It's worth noting that 5. **Fee Structures**: While exchange wallets offer convenience in trading, they often come at a cost.

Transaction fees, deposit fees, and withdrawal fees can accumulate, particularly if you're an active trader. It's crucial to understand each exchange's fee structure to ensure it doesn't erode your investment returns significantly.

Is an Exchange Wallet the Right Choice for You?

Deciding whether an exchange wallet suits your needs is contingent upon your objectives and risk tolerance.

If your primary aim is convenience and you engage in frequent trading, an exchange wallet may be ideal. The seamless integration allows for rapid response to market conditions, and the user-friendly interface can simplify portfolio management.

In real life, Conversely, if privacy, self-control, and security are your top priorities, you may wish to explore non-custodial wallets.

These wallets provide you complete access to your private keys and increased control over your digital assets, at the expense of added responsibility for securing your funds.

Best Practices for Using Exchange Wallets

To mitigate risks while using exchange wallets, consider adopting the following best practices:

It's worth noting that - **Diversify Wallet Usage**: Instead of storing all your cryptocurrencies on an exchange, use a combination of custodial and non-custodial wallets.

Keep only the amount you actively trade on the exchange and store the rest in a secure hardware wallet.

- **Enable Security Features**: Activate all available security features, such as two-factor authentication, and regularly update your login credentials.

Monitor your account activities for any suspicious transactions.

- **Stay Informed on Exchange Security Practices**: Research the exchange's history and current security protocols.

Opt for exchanges that are transparent about their security measures and asset insurance policies.

To be honest, - **Beware of Phishing Scams**: Always double-check URLs and emails purporting to be from exchanges.

Cyber threats often exploit users' unawareness or carelessness in matters of security.

Navigating the world of crypto wallet exchanges involves weighing convenience against control.

By understanding the pros and cons, you can make an informed decision that aligns with your financial strategy and risk profile. In the dynamic and unpredictable landscape of cryptocurrency, the key to successful asset management lies in staying informed and vigilant.

Chapter 17: Tax Implications: Reporting and Regulations

Understanding the tax implications of cryptocurrency transactions is crucial for anyone wishing to store and secure their crypto assets responsibly.

As governments and regulatory bodies worldwide continue to refine their frameworks concerning digital currencies, having a comprehensive understanding of these regulations is more important than ever. The following chapter will delve into the intricacies of reporting and regulations associated with cryptocurrency holdings and transactions.

Cryptocurrency as Property

The U. S. Internal Revenue Service (IRS) and many other tax authorities globally classify cryptocurrencies as property, not currency.

This designation has profound implications for how cryptocurrency transactions are taxed. Instead of treating crypto transactions as simple currency exchanges, they are considered capital transactions. Each transaction may result in a capital gain or loss, impacting your tax obligations.

Capital Gains and Losses

Just like stocks and other investment properties, when you sell or trade cryptocurrency, the difference between your purchase price (the cost basis) and the selling price is a capital gain or loss.

If you sell your cryptocurrency for more than you paid for it, you have a capital gain. Conversely, if you sell it for less, you incur a capital loss.

It's worth noting that Capital gains are further categorized based on the holding period.

If you held the cryptocurrency for more than a year, it's classified as a long-term capital gain, generally taxed at a lower rate. Conversely, if held for a year or less, it falls under short-term capital gains, taxed at your ordinary income rate.

Reporting Obligations

Individuals engaged in cryptocurrency transactions are obligated to report these activities accurately on their tax returns.

This includes transactions such as trading, selling, and converting cryptocurrencies. Even using cryptocurrencies to purchase goods and services can trigger a taxable event.

Reporting Tools

A variety of software options are available to help automate the process of tracking and reporting cryptocurrency transactions.

These tools connect with your wallets and exchanges, compiling detailed records necessary for tax reporting. By leveraging these technologies, you can ensure precise record-keeping, which is crucial for compliance.

International Regulatory Landscape

As strange as it sounds, Different countries have adopted varying approaches to the taxation of cryptocurrencies.

Understanding the local regulations where you reside or operate is essential.

United States

In the U. S.

, the IRS has issued guidance since 2014 on cryptocurrency taxation and has continued to refine its stance. As a resident or citizen, you are required to report your crypto holdings and any related income annually. The IRS treats using cryptocurrency for purchases, mining cryptocurrencies, and earning them as a form of payment or reward all as taxable events.

European Union

The tax treatment of cryptocurrency in the EU varies between member states.

Many regard cryptocurrencies as subject to capital gains tax, with details differing across jurisdictions. Some countries may have more favorable tax treatment than others, which necessitates a tailored approach for those owning and trading cryptocurrencies within the EU.

Other Countries

In real life, Each country has its regulatory stance.

For example, Japan considers cryptocurrencies as legal property and subjects them to capital gains tax. On the other hand, countries like Portugal have adopted more favorable tax strategies, exempting individuals from capital gains taxes on cryptocurrency transactions.

Keeping Abreast with Regulations

The tax rules governing cryptocurrencies are fluid, with governments continually updating their regulations as the digital currency landscape evolves.

Therefore, staying informed about changes to tax laws and regulations in your jurisdiction is paramount.

Professional Advice

Consulting a tax professional who specializes in cryptocurrency can provide personalized guidance tailored to your circumstances.

They can help you understand your reporting obligations and develop effective strategies to manage your tax liability.

Record-Keeping Best Practices

As strange as it sounds, Maintaining precise and extensive records of every cryptocurrency transaction is essential.

These records will aid in accurate reporting and could be invaluable during an audit.

Essential Records

The kind of records to keep include transaction dates, amounts, involved parties, and the purpose of the transaction.

Keeping a spreadsheet or using specialized tracking software can streamline this process.

Wallet Management

Understanding the distinctions between types of wallets—hot, cold, custodial, and non-custodial—is also crucial for tax reporting.

Each wallet type has different implications depending on its use and accessibility.

Penalties for Non-Compliance

I've seen this happen before: Tax authorities worldwide are increasing their scrutiny of cryptocurrency transactions.

Non-compliance with reporting obligations can result in significant penalties, ranging from fines to criminal charges for tax evasion.

IRS Crackdown

In the U. S.

, the IRS has begun to work with exchanges to collect 1099 information from them, thus reducing anonymity in transactions. Failing to report cryptocurrency transactions leaves taxpayers vulnerable to audits and ensuing penalties.

Conclusion

Cryptocurrencies represent a revolutionary shift in the world of finance, but they come with unique tax implications and regulatory requirements.

As governments worldwide endeavor to integrate these digital assets into existing legal frameworks, cryptocurrency holders must exercise due diligence in understanding and complying with their tax obligations. By keeping detailed records, utilizing reporting tools, and seeking professional advice, you can navigate the complex terrain of cryptocurrency taxation efficiently and effectively.

Chapter 18: Future-Proofing Your Crypto Wallet: Adapting to Change

In the rapidly evolving landscape of digital finance, future-proofing your crypto wallet is not just a prudent choice; it's an essential strategy. Cryptocurrencies, blockchain technologies, and associated ecosystems are advancing at an unprecedented pace.

Therefore, ensuring that your crypto wallet can withstand future developments and threats will safeguard your investments and empower you to capitalize on emerging opportunities. This chapter lays out pragmatic strategies for future-proofing your crypto wallet, emphasizing adaptability and foresight.

Understanding the Evolution of Crypto Wallets

To be honest, To future-proof effectively, understanding the trajectory of crypto wallet technology is critical.

Crypto wallets have evolved from basic storage tools to sophisticated applications offering a wide array of features, such as decentralized apps integrations, cross-chain compatibility, and enhanced security measures like multi-signature and biometric authentication.

Recognizing these trends helps anticipate future directions. As blockchain technology matures, expect further developments in interoperability, allowing seamless transactions across different cryptocurrencies.

Biometric security features, AI-driven fraud detection, and integration with the Internet of Things (IoT) could become standard. Thus, selecting a wallet provider that is forward-thinking and has a track record of innovation is crucial.

Selecting the Right Wallet Type

I've seen this happen before: The first step in future-proofing lies in choosing the correct type of wallet for your needs. Hardware wallets, with their offline nature, provide robust security against online threats, but keeping them updated is vital.

Software wallets, whether mobile or desktop-based, should remain current with security patches and feature upgrades. Multi-currency wallets, which support multiple blockchain networks, offer flexibility and are a wise choice for a diversified portfolio.

Evaluate whether your current wallet can be easily augmented or replaced to integrate new technologies, such as support for emerging blockchains or digital assets like Non-Fungible Tokens (NFTs).

This adaptability ensures you'll remain at the forefront of the crypto economy without needing a complete system overhaul.

Keeping Security Top-of-Mind

As strange as it sounds, In future-proofing any digital asset, security should be paramount.

Crypto wallets are prime targets for sophisticated cybercriminals who employ ever-evolving methods. To mitigate risks, employ a layered security strategy.

1. **Regular Updates:** Ensure your wallet's software is routinely updated.

Updates often include patches for vulnerabilities, thus protecting against the latest threats. Set reminders to check for updates manually if your wallet does not do so automatically.

2.

Two-Factor Authentication (2FA): This adds an essential layer of security, especially for software wallets. Look for wallets that offer 2FA or other advanced security features like biometric verification.

In real life, 3. **Cold Storage:** For long-term holdings, consider moving significant assets to cold storage solutions, which keep private keys offline.

4.

Backup Strategies: Regular backups of your wallet and private keys are essential. Store these backups securely, preferably offline, in multiple locations to prevent loss due to hardware failure or other physical threats.

Adopting Scalable Solutions

Many people don't realize this, but A critical aspect of future-proofing involves scalability—the ability to grow or adapt without performance loss.

As your investment grows, your crypto wallet must handle increased transaction volumes and larger asset allocations.

1.

Structural Flexibility: Evaluate whether your wallet supports future additions like new cryptos or emerging technologies. Open-source wallets, which benefit from community-driven development, can quickly adapt to technological advancements.

2.

Transaction Speed and Fees: With the expectation of increased blockchain usage, transaction speeds and associated fees may fluctuate. Opt for wallet services that provide variable fee options to optimize costs based on network conditions.

I've seen this happen before: 3.

Interoperability: As cross-chain transactions and decentralized finance (DeFi) grow, wallets facilitating seamless integration across platforms will be beneficial. Ensure your wallet is poised for such connectivity expansions.

Embracing Regulatory Changes

Regulation in the cryptocurrency sphere is tightening worldwide.

Keeping abreast of regulatory obligations is imperative for future-proofing. Non-compliance can lead to frozen assets or legal issues.

1. **Compliance Features:** Use wallets that integrate compliance tools relevant to your jurisdiction, such as tax reporting functionalities or Know Your Customer (KYC) processes.

2. **Stay Informed:** Subscribe to updates from credible crypto regulatory bodies or legal advisories to remain aware of changes affecting your digital assets.

3. **Portfolio Transparency:** Increasing regulatory scrutiny may demand more transparent portfolio holdings. Choose wallets facilitating reporting and tracking features to ensure regulatory readiness.

Leveraging Community Knowledge

Being part of the crypto community can offer insights into upcoming trends and advancements.

Engaging in forums, attending webinars, and following influential industry voices provide valuable information for future-proofing your crypto endeavors.

1.

Network Engagement: Regularly participate in discussions on platforms like Reddit or specialized crypto forums such as Bitcointalk. Networking with other users can provide tips and warnings about wallet issues or emerging threats.

To be honest, 2.

Educational Resources: Continuous learning through reputable sources about advancements in crypto technology is crucial. Popular online courses, podcasts, and expert panels can provide critical knowledge for future-proofing strategies.

3.

Feedback Channels: Actively engage with wallet providers to express your needs and learn about imminent features or enhancements. Providers with responsive support and strong community focus tend to adopt user-driven improvements.

Conclusion

At first glance, As the cryptocurrency realm continues its relentless advance, preparing your wallet for future challenges and opportunities is an indispensable pursuit.

By focusing on security, scalability, compliance, and community engagement, you can tailor a future-proofed strategy to ensure your digital investments remain secure and agile. Remember, the key to enduring success in the crypto world lies in the ability to adapt; by embracing change, you position yourself advantageously for all that lies ahead.

Chapter 19: Troubleshooting Common Wallet Issues

Navigating the world of cryptocurrency is akin to endeavoring into uncharted territories of modern finance and technology. While this journey offers numerous opportunities, it also presents unique challenges, especially when it comes to wallet-related issues.

As a cryptocurrency user, your wallet acts as the interface for managing and securing your digital assets. Understanding how to troubleshoot common wallet issues is crucial for ensuring seamless operations and the safety of your funds. This chapter will guide you through some of the most frequent issues users encounter and provide practical solutions to overcome these challenges.

1. Recovery Phrase and Private Key Issues

I've seen this happen before: The recovery phrase and private key are the backbone of access to your wallet.

Losing them means losing access to your funds, potentially permanently. It's crucial to store them securely, but users often face issues like misplaced keys, loss of accessibility, or compromised information.

- **Solution**: Always ensure you have multiple backups of your recovery phrase—stored in several secure locations (preferably offline).

If you believe your recovery phrase or private key has been compromised, immediately move your funds to a new wallet with a new recovery phrase or key. Regularly verify access through your backup credentials to ensure they are accurate.

2. Transaction Errors

Believe it or not, Transaction errors are a common nuisance in the world of cryptocurrency.

Whether it's a delay, a failed transaction, or confusion over transaction fees, these issues can be frustrating.

- **Solution**: First, check the status of your transaction on a reliable blockchain explorer using the transaction ID (TxID). Delays often occur due to network congestion, which might require you to wait or adjust transaction fees to expedite processing.

Ensure that you have correctly entered the receiving address to avoid irreversible mistakes. Some wallet interfaces allow you to "speed up" or "cancel" pending transactions if they haven't been confirmed, though success can vary depending on the blockchain network.

3. Wallet Connectivity Problems

Interestingly enough, Many users face connectivity issues, particularly with software wallets. This can prevent you from accessing your funds at crucial times.

- **Solution**: Start by ensuring your internet connection is stable. If the problem persists, check for updates to your wallet application—developers frequently release updates to fix bugs and improve connectivity.

If you're using a web-based wallet, clearing your browser cache or trying a different browser might resolve the issue. For hardware wallets, ensure the firmware is updated and cables are securely connected.

4. Compatibility Issues with Updates

It's worth noting that New updates to software wallets occasionally lead to compatibility issues, especially with older operating systems or hardware.

- **Solution**: Before updating any software, verify that your system supports the new version. Keeping your system software updated will minimize conflicts.

If issues arise post-update, visiting user forums or support pages related to your wallet can offer insights from others who have experienced similar problems. Rolling back to a previous version is sometimes necessary, but ensure you back up your wallet data beforehand.

5. Forgotten Passwords

The nature of crypto wallets means that password recovery is not as straightforward as traditional systems.

Many users mistakenly assume they can reset their password through standard methods.

- **Solution**: Use your recovery phrase or seed to restore access to your wallet.

Regularly test your backup methods to ensure they work and maintain a secure written record of passwords in a safe location. Consider using password managers, especially those with strong encryption, to store complex passwords securely.

6. Synchronization and Loading Issues

It's worth noting that Some wallets require synchronization with the blockchain to function correctly, and issues in this process can lead to incomplete loading or faulty synchronization.

- **Solution**: Ensure you're on a reliable and fast network connection. Sometimes, restarting the wallet application or your device can resolve sync issues.

Check wallet settings, as some might have specific synchronization options that you can adjust. If the problem persists, consulting customer support or the wallet's help section might provide targeted solutions.

7. Security Breaches and Phishing Scams

Security breaches, including phishing scams, target your wallet information, potentially leading to fund theft.

- **Solution**: Always double-check website URLs and email senders for authenticity. Never input your recovery phrase or passwords on suspicious sites.

Enable two-factor authentication (2FA) wherever possible, and stay informed about common scams and phishing tactics. Utilize wallets with strong encryption standards and consider dedicated security software to detect and block threats.

8. Multi-Signature Wallet Issues

Believe it or not, Multi-signature wallets enhance security by requiring multiple parties to authorize transactions.

However, they can also lead to complications if disagreements arise among signatories or if one party becomes unavailable.

- **Solution**: Establish clear communication channels and agreements between all parties before implementing a multi-signature scheme.

Prepare contingency plans for scenarios like a trusted party becoming uncommunicative, such as having additional signatories or employing smart contracts for pre-defined conditions.

9. Lack of Customer Support

Many people don't realize this, but One significant challenge with cryptocurrency wallets, especially lesser-known ones, is the absence of immediate customer support, which can lead to unresolved issues.

- **Solution**: Prefer wallets with an established reputation for customer support.

Engage with community forums or social media groups dedicated to your wallet; experienced users or developers often frequent these platforms and can offer practical advice. Take advantage of any available official documentation or FAQ sections, which might address your issue.

In conclusion, while wallet issues can be distressing, they are often solvable with the right approach and resources.

Maintaining diligence and adopting proactive strategies, as discussed throughout this chapter, will empower you to handle common wallet issues like a pro. As the cryptocurrency landscape continues to evolve, keeping informed and adaptive will ensure you remain at the forefront of secure digital asset management.

Chapter 20: Conclusion: Becoming a Crypto Storage Expert

As we come to the conclusion of our journey into the intricate world of crypto wallets, it is imperative to consolidate the knowledge gained into actionable expertise.

To become a discerning expert in the realm of cryptocurrency storage, meticulous understanding and mastery of the essentials are paramount. This chapter aims to cement your status as a crypto storage expert by emphasizing the critical aspects that should govern your strategies and decisions.

Embracing the Fundamentals

To be honest, An expert's proficiency is rooted in an unwavering grasp of the basics.

As you've learned, a crypto wallet is not merely a digital purse; it is a sophisticated tool designed to interact with the broader cryptocurrency network. Regardless of whether you're using a software wallet or a hardware solution, the underpinning principle remains the same: the wallet's primary function is to store your private keys securely, enabling you to manage and protect your digital assets.

Recognizing the types of wallets—ranging from hot to cold, and custodial to non-custodial—empowers you to choose the right tool for your needs.

Remember, hot wallets are for frequent transactions and ease of access, whereas cold wallets are the go-to for long-term storage and enhanced security. The choice between custodial and non-custodial wallets pivots on the level of control and responsibility you're willing to assume.

Security Is Non-Negotiable

Believe it or not, Security is the cornerstone of crypto storage expertise. As you expand your knowledge and grow your portfolio, the vigilance against security threats must bolster.

An expert ensures that multi-factor authentication is not just an option but a standard procedure. Always favor wallets that offer robust security features, such as biometric authentication and passphrase protection.

Equally vital is the concept of backup. The mnemonic seed phrase is your lifeline, an imperative for recovery should you encounter device failure or loss.

Store this information offline, in multiple secure, discreet locations. Engage in periodic reviews of your security practices, because threats evolve, and so should your defenses.

Mastery of Wallet Management

Believe it or not, True expertise is demonstrated through efficient wallet management.

This extends beyond the mere possession of secure storage; it encompasses the seamless integration of wallets with your financial activities. Ensure that you periodically review your wallet usage and the assets held, adapting to new technologies or shifting market landscapes as necessary.

Part of being an expert entails understanding the transaction processes and potential fees associated with different wallets and blockchains.

Fine-tune your understanding of network fees, confirmation speeds, and the impact these have on your transactions. An adept expert uses this knowledge to optimize costs and ensure timely transactions.

Adapting to Technological Advancements

Cryptocurrency is an ever-evolving field, characterized by technological innovation and adaptation. As a crypto storage expert, staying abreast of these changes is non-negotiable.

Engage with communities, leverage online courses, attend conferences, and consume literature pertinent to cryptocurrency and blockchain technology. Develop a habit of lifelong learning to anticipate, understand, and integrate advancements into your storage strategies.

Legal and Ethical Considerations

An unsung aspect of mastery is the understanding and application of legal and ethical principles. Navigating the crypto ecosystem requires awareness of the regulatory frameworks within your jurisdiction and an understanding of international legal landscapes.

Strive to maintain compliance and ethical standards in your dealings, because they are pivotal in fostering trust and safeguarding your assets. An expert is not just knowledgeable, but also responsible and advocates for the legitimacy and stability of the entire ecosystem.

Leveraging Professional Tools and Communities

In the quest for expertise, embrace the plethora of tools and communities that can enhance your proficiency and security. From wallet management software to security audits, the use of professional-grade tools can streamline processes and enhance security.

Equally important is active participation in a community. Peer interactions and discussions can yield critical insights and keep you informed of emerging threats and best practices.

Future-Proof Strategies

Believe it or not, Finally, becoming an expert also means preparing for the future. We've detailed the significance of diversification and not keeping all your assets in a single wallet or type of wallet.

This principle stands particularly true in the face of unforeseen technological shifts and market turbulence. Develop strategies that account for future changes in the crypto landscape, whether they pertain to regulations, technological advancements, or market dynamics.

In conclusion, becoming a crypto storage expert is a multifaceted process that integrates knowledge, practice, and adaptation. It is about continually reinforcing one's understanding, staying vigilant against threats, and remaining adaptable to change.

As you navigate your future in cryptocurrency, remember that expertise is not a static goal but an evolving journey. The skills and insights you've acquired place you at the forefront of safeguarding the digital treasures of tomorrow. Embrace the responsibility with prudence, confidence, and a commitment to excellence.

About the Author

T. S. AVINI is a writer who believes in the power of sharing life's lessons. Having faced hardship and pain, he turned to writing as a form of self-expression and healing. Today, he pours his heart into every book, aiming to help others navigate their own struggles and find strength in vulnerability.